the flap pamphlet series

Desert Sunflowers

open, read, turn

Desert Sunflowers
the flap pamphlet series (No. 10)
Printed and Bound in the United Kingdom

Published by the flap series, 2014
the pamphlet series of flipped eye publishing
All Rights Reserved

Cover Design by Petraski
Series Design © flipped eye publishing, 2010

ISBN-13: 978-1-905233-44-1
Editorial work for this series is supported by the Arts Council of England

LOTTERY FUNDED

Desert Sunflowers

Rowyda Amin

Contents | *Desert Sunflowers*

Genius Loci

Rubbing my rhubarb in Washington Square, the infamous but
much-loved wearer of woollen hats in hot weather, the wonder
dog, lamper of gold-dust drudgers, champ of wild-goose pursuits,
I, the one man band, clockless animal, whistling Tarzan, crap in
the grass, rapture dalliance on benches, chuckle in my yellow
beard a fuzz of tasty syllables. My drinking glass, my hand
I raise to Bird Man, pigeons on his shoulders, blues harp in
his lips to acclaim the wide-mouthed tulips' velveteen wine
and Kool-Aid hues; to bronze Guiseppe's pill-box, sarcastic
squirrels mocking tourists from on top; but not those green
Visigoths, the singalongers peddling gods. I'll take real figs and
not their painted ones. And you, stoic lunch-hour zebra
bent at your tuna sandwich, shrink-wrapped in pinstriped
wool for the daily auto-da-fé: do you question that I am cobalt
to the blood, a rain charmer, frog prince for a nickel with
cocksure loll, human with the composition of smoke? I shoulder
the kiloton of cogitation, the torture of dayglo tigers padding
nonstop my yellow sleeps; but to any tethered chimp that
pities me my leper life, I proffer this garden cosmopolis,
its stores of salt and creamsicle, lucid dreamers with eyes wide.

Mojave

They saw themselves walking toward themselves
over peacock-feather lakes that weren't there,
but they or their reflections disappeared
within touching distance. Father got drunk
using up the booze from the cabin to piss
pleas for help in the sand, but no planes swooped
before it dried. The sand serrated Mother's
eyelids so that she wept rose-tinted tears
that dripped into the daughter's open mouth.
In the morning, they found the girl floating
upside down in the air.
                          They prised open
her mouth and she vomited weeds and fish
that became lizards and hid in the sand.
They buried her and piled up stones
to keep her from floating away. Under the ground,
she listened to the scaly whisperings
of the lizards. Her tongue attuned to the salt
of distant lakes. She grew large, sub-divided,
hatched herself and scattered across the surface
in twelve directions while Mother and Father
crawled on their elbows through the sand,
following themselves in a circle, their bodies
fusing mouth to anus in a writhing ring
as the snake of their mirages swallowed its tail.

Ex-lover with Seaweed

Is that you on the shore,
 wearing a mask of seaweed
and a wet suit,
slick and dark green?
It looks slimy and is swarming
with tiny fleas that hop
up and down
but never leave your orbit.
You seem to be suffering
in your kelp suit,
you don't know
how you got wrapped into it, tight
as the bandages on a burn victim
but you lift a corner and pull
to show me it's not coming off.
You tug at the mask
but the rubbery green
 is flush with your lips.
The seaweed owns you like a new name.
I can't help you, I say
as you hold out
your palm blistering with airbladders.
Your tongue is a green strand
swishing from your mouth,
but the voice is lost.

Time Buries Us

I need to smell their saffron
so I drag them
out of the earth like soggy bags

hold them to me
mulchy and stained

rotten leaves steeped past yellow
in the dirt

their skulls like a smoker's
once-white ceiling.

I want to dredge their graves
for the crockery broken
in back gardens

split the soil's richness to open
the ruby caches of money spiders and find

the turmeric twist of smoke
from my grandfather's shed that I know

is down there if I dig on
past the chattering
of all the daffodil teeth.

In the Floating World

Lovers bind her wrists with bracelets shaped
after the heads and necks of swans.
The favoured birds of this city are water fowl.

The bed is always damp when she climbs into it,
a taint of must on her skin. Her dreams
are of submergence, stairways drowned in silt.

Daytimes, looking for the sea into which the canals flow,
she goes to untangle the alleyways and bridges
that knit the islands of nacre-slick stone.

When she reaches the docks, she will embark
for a city in which the avenues radiate neat as spider-silk,
where water is locked in aquifers and aloes regular as crystal.

All she carries: on her right hand, an untethered peregrine.
She sings to it as her path circles, a wordless barcarole.

Night Work

From your bed, noctilucent paths
are rambling, one of which could lead
through the Tudor knot of yew hedge
to that rose arbour at its centre
where white-slippered sleep is breathing.

Simple to untangle one path after the next
if you still had all night, but fat mice
are eating through the blue and green wool
with which the maze is tapestried.

Though tawny owls, silver-beaked, dive
to unpick the plump bodies, bursting
every pink and yellow cross-stitch,
you're still awake at dawn, tattered
in your threadbare nest of bones.

Out of Line

Her eyebrows indicated an ergotistic dreamer.
Why's she looking, he thought, so like a fire
in the gold souk?

His eyes were benzene rings circling
two fig trees. Jackdaws at the tear ducts
beat ash with black feathers.

Half-cut on Waldorf pharmaceuticals, she trailed
gator-hemmed biography. He could say
she was tame, no hipster maniac shredding euphoric quince.

He looked bunkum, grafted from his father's tongue,
an oryx mooncalf sitting cubicle zazen.
Sunset flamboyance in the gym, his skin exquisite tartrazine.

She'd have money, rooms of mirrorwork mandrils,
a hex-filled ossuary for her begetter matrons.
That rosy cab-girl speech, all 'Kiss my glove' and curfews.

He kept, no doubt, some soignée Venusian dispenser
of gemmy smiles and flaked wheat.
Kittenfingered witch, a cosmetic masterpiece.

Her voice would sing 'Zelzela, shwee shwee',
all about the asp and the paper cut.
Her tarot sign an eye-green malkin, electrified shred of mink.

Dear Ludovic

The wards are arranged according to the constellations, my bed in
the upper pan of Libra. My elderly neighbour cat-sleeps to avoid the
mother who hovers over his bed like marsh gas, moueing because
he won't leave with her. There's little to admire through the window
besides the garden and that is pocked by grave robbers rooting up
nasturtiums in search of plastic bangles.

The small nurse with the Nefertiti eyes comes by every six clicks on
the morphine drip, swinging a brain-hook with panache. She doesn't
like my writing but never intervenes, more worried by the bird-headed
man seen looking in through the third-floor windows of the cafeteria.

You should've been here for the masked ball in the pathology lab
when the surgeons came as surgeons, the nurses as nurses and
the pathologists, giggling, as a group of sanitation inspectors with
laminated name tags. The test tube reliquaries gave a heart- warm glow
when the minute came to give each other mouth-to-mouth. Ever since,
they can't stop flirting. The locum overdosed me three times, licking
her cherry vanilla lips at the ward sister.

Of the Old Man of the Mountain

We were both bored, sitting on a wall when he
picked us up. His chauffeur drove for hours, too far
to change our minds and ask to be taken back,
up fenceless mountain roads to the gates
of a white villa hidden in low clouds and cedars.

The old man peeled oranges and poured retsina.
Leaning on cushions, he lit a glass pipe
and we watched the smoke curl into its stem.
He breathed the smoke from his mouth into ours
and stroked our hair as we fell asleep listening
to him tell of the garden where we would forever
be happy and fifteen.

We woke to the sounds of silver birds chiming
in the fruit trees over our heads, their filigreed
wings glimmering between the leaves. We shook
figs and pomegranates from the orchard. From over
a lake came the sound of laughter. Boys and girls
with long hair dragged us down with them to swim
and dry off naked in the warm grass.

The old man always sat a little apart. Each night
he wound the mechanical silver birds to wake us.
When we mentioned our mothers, he touched honeyed wine
to our lips and we forgot their names.

One night he brought the pipe, kissed our mouths again
with hot smoke and we opened our eyes at the foot
of the mountain, cheeks printed with gravel,
a dead dog buzzing with flies on one side of us,
on the other the buses and scooters from the village,
drivers laughing and leaning on their horns.

Monkey Daughter

On my birthday, my mother takes delivery
of a baby capuchin. All week
she has been converting her study
into a nursery, with a cot
and yellow curtains, cupcake patterned.

She feeds the monkey
warm milk from a bottle,
little chunks of papaya and apple.
Hushes and lulls, names it Laura.
The monkey's scared brown eyes roll like olives.
I want to shake them out of the jar.

Laura wears tiny dungarees
and pinafores, my baby clothes
from the attic, where my parents
had been saving them for grandchildren.
Her photo replaces mine on the fridge.

This one, my mother says, pinning
the monkey's nappy, *will not grow up.*

Desert Sunflowers

While they waited for the weather to turn, Fermi
offered wagers on the odds of igniting

the atmosphere and destroying the earth
or just New Mexico. Teller made them nervous,

slapping on the sunscreen. Oppenheimer
wore dark glasses like the rest

and held onto a post with damp hands.
He had ten dollars on them failing.

In the control centre, Allison counted down
5-4-3-2-1 NOW! They shielded their eyes

against the flash then saw the mountains lit up
clear as noon by the orange-yellow fireball

that mushroomed blood red to pink
at ten thousand feet before it dimmed.

When it was over they blinked at their blind spots.
Isidor Rabi passed the whiskey. Bainbridge said

Now we are all sons of bitches. Oppenheimer smiled,
strutted into base camp in his wide-brimmed hat.

By night, rain was falling with the dust
and next morning they saw, all around

the green glass crater, in every section
of the Jornada del Muerto,

dense fields of black-hearted sunbursts,
blossoming between the mountains.

Zugunruhe

Yes, you've been the freckled darling
of all the rooftop cabarets,

your high kicks petalling the town
with cheap scanties – but now you're the one

left singing after the music has ended
so it's time to get the suitcase down,

pack those veneerial fripperies,
make a plan to fly south.

9 Carrot Poem

Troubling glint – swallowed goldfish
confer sub rosa.

Chrysanthemum lanterns illuminate
a silent house.

The jeunesse dorée, pinkies out,
sip ochre marmalade.

Tigers in straw
ambush martian minotaur.

Gilded girls sleep in rows,
under green lace and dandelion.

Goldbugs turn dung beetle, dig
pyritic coprolites.

Ginger-headed mummies pickle
in mandarin vats.

Votives of haw and amber
kindle under ground.

Hennaed hands torch
like Van Gogh's beard.

She Was Born

On a Saturday, during the apple season.
The villagers disagreed as to which she most resembled:
An old woman, a rocky stream, a broken horse.

She blew into the village as a cloud of ash.
Years later, the village was unearthed intact.

She waited in the forest for the village to be constructed.

It is said she is descended from two dead languages.
She has a memory of ships
and a slow journey inland.

Insect Studies

She flinched only as I began
the black frame of the Emerald Swallowtail
poised to land on a blossom of the cherry branch
that bloomed across her back.

When I'd wiped off the rust of blood
and excess colour and padded her latest with gauze,
she slipped her shirt back on
and we drank coffee
while a teenage boy searched through flash sheets
to find the right kanji for his arm.

She showed me pictures of fritillaries
she wanted inked in the spaces
on her lower back and thighs.
The boy settled on 'death'
and took her place.

See you after payday she said,
but never did except for the night in June
when I woke silver with honeydew
and she stood in the doorway,
her body a flutter of bright little wings
and antennae curling away from her
like cursive script
and the butterflies flew to me,
flattening themselves against my skin,
each eager proboscis
burying deep in the tissues.

Hunter's Moon

At forty three, Memmie le Blanc
lives by making artificial flowers,
exhibits herself to the curious
and sells them copies

of Madame Hecquet's *Histoire
d'une Jeune Fille Sauvage Trouvée
dans les Bois à l'âge de dix ans*.

She stays off the Paris streets,
folds her long tree-climbing fingers
morning and night for prayer.

When she sleeps, windows open
for the breeze, the body she holds
stiff as a nun disappears. Her toes

touch grass and she is the wild girl, quick
as a spring, who chased down a hare
and dropped it, bloody and warm,
at the Queen of Poland's feet.

Polly

The reason is first that I am a spectacle,
so they fetch me seeds and fresh water,

guard me from cats in a house of metal filigree.
For reason that my feathers spread

plumes of lapis, teal, apricot, and in the non-jungle
colours are rare and most prized;

for that I translate the sunlight into iridescence,
they have need of me.

For the second it is that my voice is more ticklish
than a creeping fig and more honey

than kapok flowers, so that they prefer to hear
their own language from my beak.

Café Danube

He stayed behind the fridge until he was sure
there was no one left, then stepped through
the litter of glass and abandoned suppers
to the podium with the Yamaha synth.
He righted the stool and played, as he did
most evenings, the themes from Love Story,
Casablanca and Titanic. Rain squalled
through the empty door frames. A dog
entered, shook itself, licked the cream
from a fallen éclair and urinated on the leg
of a waiter, which was sticking out
from behind the bar. The pianist broke
for a whiskey then switched to show tunes.
Water pooled into the centre of the room.
He heard claps, far off but getting louder.

Frost Fair

Slideshow faces flicker from the station.
You're following the mood to London Bridge
where taxis cruise black as death's pyjamas.
The Thames you find is glacier silk, shantied
with booths and carousels. Five screaming hens
speed by in a white horse sleigh. Ballad singers
busk their vagrant lines. *Alas my love, you do me wrong.*
Crowds scoff hotdogs and candyfloss,
cheer as Punch batters Judy with the baby.
Hog roasts spit fat on the ice, children watching
with faces pink and hot. *Thy girdle of gold so red.*
Falling snow feathers the whipped bear moonwalking in chains.
It looks at you with marshmallow eyes
and you want to take its arms and zip over the ice,
feel fur on your cheeks, skating against the wind to the estuary
where the ice breaks apart, but you smile, hands in pockets,
and turn to the skittles and acrobats, sugared crepes and hot wine.
And yet thou wouldst not love.

Sanatorium

So light he hardly dents the mattress, my grandfather breathes with half a lung. Moths, unseen by the nurse on night duty, flutter down from the curtains and hover over his open mouth. Feeling the breath become weak, they wind silk reins around the iron bars of the bed. They tense and tug the strings to prepare for the moment when the breathing stops. Then they will drag the wheeled bed through the double doors of the ward, out the front entrance and up, over the car park, to the hanging lightbulb of the moon.

Notes on Poems

Mojave
Some details contained in this poem were suggested by a reading of
Ordeal by Hunger: the Story of the Donner Party by George R. Stewart

Time Buries Us
'We kill time; time buries us.' From *Epitaph for a Small Winner*
by Joaquim Maria Machado de Assis , translated by William L.
Grossman.

In the Floating World
This poem was written for an installation called 'Archive' created
jointly with the visual artist Franny Swann as part of a project called
Pistols and Pollinators, which paired poets and artists for a six month
collaboration culminating in an exhibition.
'Archive' was conceived as a fantastical museum display containing
the grave goods of a woman from a fictional ancient civilisation. The
display case contained jewellery manufactured by Franny from goose
bones. The poem, evoking the woman who had worn those jewels,
served as a label for the display.

Out of Line
This poem was commissioned by the Victoria and Albert Museum
in association with The Books Project, for an event celebrating the
anthology *Ten: New Poets from Spread the Word*, edited By Bernardine
Evaristo and Daljit Nagra. The poem was written in response to a
series of photographs entitled 'Out of Line' by Jowhara Al Saud.

Of the Old Man of the Mountain
This poem draws loosely upon mythology about Rashid ad-Din Sinan.
In particular, it is influenced by Marco Polo's account of tales about
him.

Insect Studies
This poem was inspired by the information on Japanese traditional
beliefs about butterflies contained in the 'Insect Studies' chapter of
Lafcadio Hearn's *Kwaidan: Stories and Studies of Strange Things*.

Hunter's Moon
This poem was inspired by the account of Memmie Le Blanc in
Michael Newton's *Savage Girls and Wild Boys: A History of Feral
Children*.

Lightning Source UK Ltd.
Milton Keynes UK
UKHW010722210321
380690UK00002B/67

9 781905 233441